# Dealing with I

## At Work & At Home

Workbook solutions on the psychology of setting boundaries & how to deal with negative, overconfident & conceited people with arrogance & bad attitudes

Samantha Claire

ISBN-13:
978-1717231062

ISBN-10:
1717231063

# Introduction

Whether at work, in school or even at home, people are constantly having conflicts.

Conflict could arise from all manner of things, and the biggest challenge that most people face is dealing with the conflict constructively. Conflict brings out negative feelings and yet it's necessary to build intimacy in relationships. How then do you transform such a negative thing into a positive one?

Your feelings and attitude towards conflict are important, as well as how you speak your truth to a "difficult" person while still remaining fair.

It is therefore important to learn assertiveness and how to fight fair to avoid damaging the relationship.

Conflict is assumed to arise from one's interaction with an annoying person, but what of when you are the difficult person?

There are signs to look out for to determine whether one is difficult as well as ways in which one can resolve the conflict that arose from their hurtful behaviors.

Healthy boundaries determine how happy a relationship will be and knowing where to place these boundaries will make your relationships easier.

It is also important to note that conflict resolution is best learned early and there is a need to teach children the skills they need to resolve conflict and stand up for themselves.

This book will handle the above issues as well as teach you how to gain respect from those around you, including the difficult people.

## What are boundaries?

What exactly is a boundary, when it comes to relationships?

Basically, a limit that you set between yourself and the other individual; a clear place where you start and the other individual ends. Think about it as a fence in your backyard.

You are the gate keeper and get to choose who you let in, and who stays out. Who you let in the entire backyard, or who you instantly evict.

You may still be keeping them at arm's reach; however, you are also giving them a chance to show their credibility to you both physically and emotionally.

The purpose of setting a healthy boundary is, naturally, to safeguard your interests and wellbeing.

Personal boundaries, like the No Trespassing sign, specify where yours end and others start and are determined by the amount of physical and psychological space you allow in between yourself and others.

Individual boundaries assist you in deciding what kinds of communication, behavior, and interactions are acceptable.

It sends out a clear message that if you violate that boundary, there will be repercussions.

This type of boundary is easy to imagine and comprehend since you can see the sign and the territory it safeguards.

Self-boundaries can sometimes be more difficult to define or draw the line, since the lines are sometimes not obvious, can morph, and are distinct for each individual.

## Kinds of Boundaries

There are a number of places where boundaries are put into play:

- Spiritual boundaries relate to your beliefs and experiences in connection with God or a greater power.
- Physical limits relate to your personal space, privacy, and body. Do you give a handshake or a hug to whomever and when?

- Healthy psychological boundaries need clear internal limits, knowing your feelings and your responsibilities to yourself and others.

- Mental boundaries put on your thoughts, values, and opinions. Are you easily suggestible? Do you know what you think and believe, and can you hold onto your opinions? Can you listen with an open mind to another person's opinion without being demanding? If you become highly emotional, argumentative, or defensive, it's possible you have weak psychological limits.

- Material boundaries determine what you give or provide, such as your money, car, clothes, books, food, or tooth brush.

- Sexual boundaries secure your comfort level with sexual touch and activity or the what, where, when, and with whom.

## Indicators of unhealthy boundaries

These are clues that tell if you are suffering from not setting healthy boundaries. They are:

- Feeling bad or guilty when you say no.

- Falling apart so somebody can care for you.

- Not speaking up when you are dealt with badly.

- Accepting advances, touching and sex that you don't desire.

- Letting others define you.

- Taking as much as you can for the sake of taking.

- Giving as much as you can for the sake of offering.

- Expecting others to fill your needs automatically.

- Touching an individual without asking.

- Going against personal values or rights to please others.

## Setting boundaries

When you feel pain around somebody intrusive, whether they are rude or something comparable, calibrate your energies and resources accordingly. You are governed by restricted energy and time that you can invest in others. Spend time only to those who deserve you.

**Do you have difficulty setting limits?**

In any relationship (whether it is with family, partners or close friends), it is our responsibility to set the boundaries on how others treat us. Having strong boundaries is vital in securing your body, mind, and spirit.

Setting limits can make a big influence on the quality of your life too. The greatest part of boundaries setting is how powerfully, you communicate them.

You can have the healthiest set of limitations in the world, however if you do not communicate them, you are simply going to produce confusing relationships, both for you and everyone else included. When setting boundaries, it is vital to connect without blaming the other person.

Love yourself by setting specific limitations with anyone who believes it is alright to hurt, even the ones they claim to love.

It is required and healthy to set limits. It is called loving yourself! Limitations are set for your security and pride.

Not setting and imposing healthy constraints, result in co-dependent and clingy habits. Discover the power of boundaries, so that you can begin to gain respect and start being pleased with yourself. Tell those close to you that your priorities have changed and you are now taking care of your needs.

If you feel your own resistance in looking after yourself, remember, when you put yourself first, you are then better at serving others with no hidden pains or anger.

Look after your precious inner child/inner life trigger, as if it were life itself, because it is.

You are never obliged to address anybody's issues or demands if you don't wish to.

Constant requirements and demands from colleagues, co-workers, friends, and families can leave you drained and irritated.

It's not an easy thing to say no to others.

Rather than establishing your boundaries around a hard relationship in your life, you need to make your boundaries about you. They can do whatever they desire as long as they do not cross the line of your boundaries

**Important limit setting actions:**

- Self-Awareness: Determine where your borders are weak or non-existent.

- Develop new borders that honor you.

- In the start, you will most likely feel egocentric, guilty, or ashamed somewhat when you set limitations.

- Setting borders takes practice and determination.

- Hard boundaries or limits are not flexible.

You must communicate this carefully, yet firmly, to others.

When you set boundaries on your own and appreciate the limitations of others, you are actually building more powerful relationships.

Just because setting a limit with somebody becomes uncomfortable for them it does not imply we have to pull back. Remember that saying no and setting a border with violent, irresponsible, or controlling individuals is challenging their habits or the hold they think they have on you. You can set a border and focus on someone else's feelings at the same time.

You are just responsible to interacting and engaging while appreciating the border in a considerate manner.

When you determine the need to have to set a limit, do it plainly, preferably without anger and in a couple of words as possible.

Just set the border calmly, securely, plainly, and respectfully. Setting strong borders will aid you to stand up for yourself, stop agreeing to do things you truly do not want to do, and begin to feel less guilty about putting your own requirements first. There is absolutely nothing wrong in taking care of yourself.

When you do not have any limits set, other people will step over the line without even understanding where the boundary was. Demands/Requests: Warn them about possible effects, if they continue to ignore your demand.

**Implement your boundaries**

Determine which battles are worth battling and which ones you can just ignore. Set effects that affect the other individual more than you.

Regard others' limitations: Stop breaking others' limitations.

Know and be considerate of other's limits as you want them to be considerate of you.

Follow-Up: Let them know how they are doing on satisfying your demands. Continue to inform and reinforcing the message.

Reward those who are valuing your boundaries and have repercussions for the ill-mannered habits.

**Self-respect**

Typically, when respect is discussed, the concept of dealing with others the way you want to be dealt with shows up.

For some people, the reality is that we treat others better than we treat ourselves. To preserve self-respect, you need to secure your self-esteem first and then you can enjoy healthy relationships. You also have to acknowledge your need to implement and set limitations, that's why knowing and understanding your restrictions is required, as previously mentioned.

Set limits with your time and energy so you can work in the most effective way to satisfy your highly regarded goals and objectives. You can likewise manage reasonable expectations about what you can do and ask for help when you absolutely require it.

Recognize, honor and appreciate your very own needs, desires, and comfort zones. Some individuals are so concerned with trying to be kind to others; they forget to check with their own inner compass thus failing to discover and know that their own needs truly are. A requirement for respect.

The earlier you realize your own zones, the less likely you will let individuals go too far. That's why respect for self is the most crucial element to think about when it comes to creating and fostering meaningful relationships of any kind. You must love yourself, before you can love others.

Be considerate and anticipate reverence or lack thereof, both in public and at home. People who are self-important or bicker in public are self-demeaning and aggravating to be with. You absolutely must be clear on what they can and cannot do, as mentioned before.

**Respect another person's body as well as your own.**

Acting as though the other individual belongs to you leads to loss of respect, absence of enthusiasm in the relationship, and just overall, general deterioration. This doesn't always suggest asking formal permissions through words. However, look for the energy and body language that clearly says, yes.

**Don't take without asking**

Taking food off somebody s plate without asking is an example of violating personal boundaries which you should try to avoid.

People oftentimes do feel it's intimate and charming to take food off each other's plate. What's mine is yours mindset does result in closeness and intimacy but only if it's acceptable to the parties concerned and if within the defined boundaries.

**Protect your most precious resource: YOU**

Speak honestly without being too crass. Request for help when you need it, and give it when they ask. You don't have to be a superman who can do everything, to everyone, every time. Be compassionate with yourself. Likewise consider how your behavior has an effect on others. This is accomplished by setting your own boundaries while being careful not to overstep on others. Prior to speaking, believe in what you're saying and its merits. You can't just be moving your lips; you must actually believe what you're saying and take responsibility of your own behaviors.

**Don't lose yourself in a relationship**

You can love somebody without letting them in -- as unusual it might sound. The inner circle needs to be reserved for those you want to play an active part in your life and at the same time provide you support.

Pay attention to your inner self, your personal standards and wishes need to be acknowledged and respected. Before stressing on how to please them, be particular to your own needs to ensure that your individual power and space is not abused.

Accept that other people's expectations and feelings are not more important than your own. You come first! The most vital relationship -- the one you have with yourself -- sets the tone for each one of your relationships.

## Implementing boundaries

"If you call me names, I will clearly have you understand it, in no unclear terms, while I share my strong displeasure with you!"

If you continue the bad behaviors, I will reconsider my options, including leaving this relationship.

Respect their boundaries, and stop breaching theirs, and in return they should respect yours!

Sounds fair doesn't it?

When you've developed the healthy boundaries in a relationship, you also need to be consistent. Consistency is the secret for all those who deal with people in their lives, who don't respect boundaries. Eventually, they will understand your consistency and firmness.

When you set restrictions on yourself and respect the boundaries of others, you create great relationships. It is tough to set boundaries without setting consequences.

If you are setting boundaries in a relationship, and you are not yet at a point where you are prepared to leave the relationship-- then do not threaten to leave.

Never ever claim something that you are not prepared to follow through with To set limits and not implement them, provides the other person an avenue to continue walking over you! A Boundary/boundary is a dividing line that separates one place from another. Although a boundary line can be clearly marked by a fence or a highway, it is never ever totally clear precisely where one ends and the other starts.

In a comparable fashion, when we use the word Boundaries to explain limits and guidelines in relationships.

Setting boundaries is not about threats. It means providing them possible choices and consequences for the poor choices or actions they make. We cannot be in a healthy relationship without adequate boundaries.

Express with the other person exactly what you prefer in healthy, respectful relationships. A healthy boundary is not easily set up particularly if it's been years of enabling bad behaviors to persist.The purpose of setting a healthy boundary is, obviously, to safeguard and take great care of yourself.

**Emotional limitations shield your feelings from other people.**

It's like an imaginary line or force field that separates you from others.

Healthy psychological boundaries require clear internal limitations and understanding your feelings and your obligations to yourself and others.

**To set a limit with an upset person**

Use easy, direct language.

Help people understand how they can appreciate your new limits.

Verbalize your boundaries clearly such as; "If you continue, I'll need to leave the room."

The biggest part of setting limitations is HOW clearly you communicate it to them.

You can have the healthiest set of boundaries in the world, though if you do not communicate them clearly, you are going to develop some truly challenging relationships.

Learn to say no to excess responsibilities:

"Although this company is crucial to me, I need to decline your request for more volunteer work because I need to acknowledge my family's needs, and spend more quality time them. "

I'll need to sleep on it; I have a policy of not deciding immediately."


Requests:

Calmly tell people exactly what you need them to stop doing or start doing.

Get their promise in acknowledging your requests.

Accept that we cannot change others.

We are excused and unaffected from what comes out of their mouths.

We are not responsible for the daily choices they make or their reactions, and

so on.

The bottom line?

Because you cannot alter other people, change how you perceive them!

Boundary setting is not about getting other people to change (regardless of

the fact that at the start, it could appear as that). It's truly about picking what

you will and won't endure any longer in your life.

Boundaries are required in becoming a healthy mature person, and stabilizing

your work and personal life effectively.


With the awareness that I may alter my circumstance by changing myself, I

discovered an extraordinary power in learning how to develop limitations

with men and women who disrespected and mistreated me. Those who mistreat themselves and others are not going to change unless they truly intend to and generally by getting professional help to do so. Only by leaving bad relationships did my circumstance change for the better, regardless of the fact that theirs did not.

## Speaking your truth in difficult situations

When dealing with difficult people, there are 4 ways that you can go about it. You could choose to do nothing and endure the bad treatment. The downside is that you suffer and get frustrated and hurt. The complaining to your friends can drive people away. You could also choose confrontation, where you deal with the person causing you difficulty directly. This could get ugly. In addition, you may choose to change your attitude and mindset towards the bad treatment. Finally, you may choose to just walk away. When the situation is not worth resolving and if it keeps getting worse, walking away is the best thing to do.

## Confrontation

There's a point in every tough predicament, when you understand you're bothered.

In that minute, the primitive part of your brain is provided with 2 options, fight or flight. You can choose to either confront the individual or forget it. When someone has in fact hurt us, we will bring that pain within us, until we can find a way to forgive the other person or until he changes.

We might believe we are striking back for wrongs done to us if we fail to forgive, but holding onto that animosity hurts us much more than the other person. An important step toward forgiveness can be to face someone who has hurt you. Calling out someone on their BS or bad habits can feel real good, but at the same time may cause a lot of trouble.

It's easy to get frustrated with others, nevertheless make sure you're picking your battles wisely. If you're just quibbling silly little things, you're going to come across as a normal jerk.

When we are irritated by someone's bad habits towards us, it's common to dislike that person. While this is natural, it can make the most harmless events appear irritating.

**Do a self-check**

Is it the particular habits, that's bothering you or is it something about that person's character? If it's the latter, then identify exactly what it is that they are doing that's annoying you. While you might not like the guy, it's seldom useful to attack any person for no good reason.

Know what lies at the heart of your headaches.

While one can say that being distressed is a type of harm, use that as the base test for when to face someone who might be harmful.

That being said, it's a great idea to define "harm" as something that triggers you to experience an immediate negative effect (i.e.. it disrupts your sleep, it costs you to lose money, other difficulties and so on).

Get your problem details in order, and confront the person, when you're not upset.

Follow the following steps:

**Choose your battles**

You don't have to address everything that upsets you.

If the issue at hand is likely to have a negative impact on your relationship if not handled, then address it.

If you can live without bringing up the issue and if raising the issue could upset you further, and the relationship is not that significant-- just let it go.

**Take a pause**

When upset, breath, collect your thoughts and then respond when you are calmed down. Responding in the heat of the moment could result in actions that you will regret. Pausing to collect your thoughts will keep your relationships intact.

**Clearly state the issues that upset you**

Be assertive in your communication and don't give the offender room to manipulate or belittle your feelings.

Make use of 'I' instead of 'you' statements to eliminate instances where the other person goes on defense.

Be polite

Being upset is not an excuse to name call or shout.

Calm yourself down and resist the urge to sink down to their level.

The calmer and more polite you are, the more likely the other person will mirror your behavior and become polite as well.

**Stick to the facts**

State the issues that upsets you, without using too much emotion. The other person may not understand why you are upset and you don't need to convince him.

Simply state the facts and move on without engaging in arguments.

**Minimize your interactions**

When a person keeps upsetting you, limit the amount of time spent with the person.

## Seek mediation

Where the difficult person is a person you can't avoid like a colleague; find someone who can mediate to improve the situation.

## Change your mindset

Difficult people will always be there

No matter where you live or work, there will always be people who end up hurting others over and over.

Since you can't avoid or transform all the difficult people in your life, knowing their traits can make it easier to anticipate their actions and minimize the hurt and agitation. Hostile people thrive as bullies and will rarely acknowledge mistakes. Rejection-sensitive people are hard to talk to, as they get offended by anything. Neurotic people thrive on criticism. They always seem to find fault in other people.

Egoists live by the principle 'my way or the highway!' They don't appreciate compromise.

## Don't be easily offended

Since you can't control the other person's behavior, control your reactions and perception of it.

Stretch yourself and reduce the instances where you get angry and lose your cool.

**Examine your own behavior**

If you find yourself dealing with the same types of people; evaluate your role in their behaviour.

Find out why you attract certain types of people and the things you could be doing that trigger certain reactions.

Develop your self-awareness to help you handle difficult people better in the future.

**Be aware of how you perceive others**

What appears as difficulty in a person could simply be a personality difference, or a friend who is going through a hard time. Instead of judging others, try putting yourself in their shoes. If you empathize with others, you will find that you no longer get offended by their actions.

**When you are the difficult person**

We all hope to minimize encounters with difficult people but what if you are the difficult one?

Here are a few signs that you could be a difficult person. You have few work friends

If your connections at work are all work related and you find yourself without people to go for lunch with or chat on personal matters, you may be considered difficult by your colleagues.

To know where you stand for sure, seek feedback from your co-workers.

Once you receive feedback, try making some changes and then observe how your relationships go.

## Your self-worth is low

If you feel like your co-workers don't respect you, you could become defensive or withdrawn.

This in turn makes you appear difficult.

To overcome this; participate in things that you are good as they will shift your focus from the negative to positive and help you open up as opposed to being withdrawn or defensive.

## People leave you out

If your colleagues have activities that they regularly undertake without you or you are never included in information sharing; it might be a signal that they find you difficult. Most people choose to avoid difficult people over confrontation and you may never receive feedback if you are considered difficult.

To overcome this, seek out feedback and when you get unsolicited feedback, seriously consider it.

Feedback will help you make changes if you take time to understand where the problem is.

## If you are always complaining

We all complain from time to time but if you find yourself complaining all the time and having more bad days than good ones, something is off.

People are drawn to happy people and if you complain most of the time, they will avoid you or simply turn a deaf ear.

Cultivate positivity by paying attention to your thoughts before you verbalize them.

Speak positive things and where there is nothing positive to say, choose silence.

## You keep blowing up

While anger is a normal reaction when people interfere with what we are passionate about; frequent anger that is triggered by many situations and many people is a problem.

Difficult people blow up due to bottled frustration and seem to be at war with several co-workers.

If you fall in the above category, determine the source of your issues and practice anger management.

## You feel like everyone is against you

If everyone seems to have an agenda against you, the reaction is to build walls and create distance.

This in turn makes you appear difficult.

Instead of creating walls, find trustworthy people to talk to and determine whether your concerns are real as opposed to shutting everyone out.

**Your performance reviews reveal that you are difficult**

Your supervisor may tell you directly or indirectly that they find you difficult.

If you notice something in your performance review alluding to the fact that you are difficult, don't ignore it.

Seek more information and ask for specific instances that led to the conclusion.

Once you understand why you are considered difficult, ask for suggestions on how to better handle the different situations.

## Resolving conflict that you caused

**Confirm what you really want**

Before scheduling a conversation with the person that you've offended, determine what you really want the conversation to achieve. If you truly want to resolve the issue at hand, examine your emotions to determine if you a really in the right state to handle the conversation.

**Understand what actually happened**

Determine if the issue was a clear wrong or simply a grey area. Go over what happened and determine what you really need to apologize for.

**Handle your feelings first**

Sometimes even when it's clear you are the one on the wrong, you may still not feel apologetic. Some people use aggression or defence to disguise the shame they feel. Don't let other feelings cloud the situation, when wrong just apologize. Apologizing makes you the bigger person and the relationship is much more valuable than your pride and reputation.

**Get into the other person's shoes**

Step out of your hurt for a moment and try and see the situation from the other person's perspective. When you shift the focus from yourself to the other person, your feelings no longer seem that important. You may feel wronged and hurt but a change in perspective helps you realize that the relationship matters more than being right.

**Make a list of reasons why you need to make amends**

Writing things down makes it easier to interpret. Write the wrong that you did and where the blame is shared, make a note of it as well. Once you've written the reasons down, go over them to see if anything leaps out. Writing down can help you identify patterns and you can use that to determine the motivation behind the actions.

## Make amends when your heart is clear

If you still feel angry and defensive, postpone the conversation. Apologizing when you have too much emotional baggage will make the apology appear insincere as it will actually be insincere.

## Decide how you'll make up for the wrong that you did

Move past your shame and come up with ways to make up for the wrongs you committed. Making amends is different for everyone and only you know when your actions are sincere. Sometimes, it requires going beyond an apology to taking action.

## Determine what you'll say

Rehearse the conversation beforehand. Go over the list of reasons that you made, come up with ways you could have handled things differently and give a way forward. It is important to remember that a mere sorry won't cut it. Take responsibility for what you did, explaining exactly what you did wrong. In addition, explain how you intend to act going forward in order to prevent the mistake from happening again.

### Apologize in person

Making amends in person shows your willingness to be in direct contact with the person again.

### Prioritize the apology

When you meet the other person, begin with the apology. The aim is to restore the relationship so avoid accusatory statements like 'you' statements and instead use 'I think' and 'I feel' statements. Furthermore, resist the temptation to justify your statements as that will undo the apology.

### Make it quick and simple

Make your points clear and short. A long apology simply double backs itself

### Allow the other person to vent

Grant the other person space to air their grievances. Their perceptions may be wrong and unjustified but they have a good reason for feeling the way they feel. In addition, listen keenly in order to understand what actually hurt them

### Provide restitution

In addition to making a genuine apology, back it up with action. Explain how you intend to change your behaviour, explain what the situation taught you and give the other person some power to act should you fail to keep your promise. You could also ask the other person to tell you how they feel amends should be made.

**Avoid future mistakes**

Do your best to avoid repeating the mistake. Hurting a person the same way twice is a sure way to erode trust.

**Move on**

Wallowing in self-pity won't add any value to your life. Forgive yourself and move on with your life regardless of the other person's reaction.

## What you can control in conflict

When dealing with a difficult person, you may feel drained and like you are losing your sanity. While you can't control the other person, there are certain things you can control.

**Your future plans**

Instead of focusing on the conflict and the negative feelings that arise due to a difficult work environment, focus on why you need to remain there or make plans to exit. Knowing where you want to be in the future takes the focus from the current difficult situation.

**Your perspective**

You can be so wrapped up in conflict especially where the difficult colleague presents difficulty on a daily basis. Instead of letting your days be dull and negative, you could change your attitude towards the conflict. A change of attitude can help you realize that the disagreement is not that significant after all and you thus don't need to lose your joy because of it.

## Your reaction

You cannot control the other person's responses no matter how hard you try. All you'll get is frustration. Instead of shouting in response to the other person's raised voice, remain calm. Choose who you want to be and be that person even when your buttons are pressed. Being the bigger person will leave you more satisfied than if you got into the mud with them.

## Your investment

Consider the level of investment that you've made in the conflict. If you spend your time thinking, talking and engaging in the conflict instead of focusing on your work, there's a problem. Focus on your work more than the conflict and reduce your investment in the drama.

## Your responsibility in the conflict

In most circumstances, conflict is not one sided. It takes two to keep a conflict going. Examine your role in the conflict and seek ways to change. If you change and no longer participate in the conflict, it will diminish.

**Your hopes**

Examine your expectations to find out whether they contribute to the conflict. You may be holding unreasonable expectations for yourself and possibly do the same to others. When they are unfulfilled, frustration sets in and you may perceive your colleagues as difficult. Change your expectations especially where you measure the performance of others against your personal preferences and your frustrations will decrease.

**Your energy**

You can choose the amount of energy to put in the conflict. If you give it 110 percent of yourself, you'll have nothing left to give other areas of your life and this could result in other failed relationships.

**Your way of dealing with it**

The way you process conflict determines your mood and reactions. If you don't know how to positively process the hurt, seek the help of a counsellor or a trusted person.

**Who you are**

Sometimes people blow up and damage items in the name of being offended. When you make poor decisions because someone hurt you, you are giving them control over your morality. Choose to meet your obligations and maintain your good character even when the other person tries to make you stoop low.

## Resolving conflict at the workplace

Conflict at the workplace is inevitable due to miscommunication, dishonesty or too much honesty, poor work habits, employee attitudes, insubordination, poor treatment of others among other issues. To successfully handle conflict at the work place you need to do the following:

**Acknowledge different points of view**

Every individual looks at the world differently based on values, culture and personal history. Understanding where each individual is coming from will help you resolve issues better as the issue behind the issue is easy to recognize.

**Recognize emotions in others**

Emotions both negative and positive are a window into discovering people's personal values. Most managers, however, only acknowledge the positive emotions but fail to take into account the negative ones. Positive emotions are an indicator of fulfilled expectations whereas negative ones suggest that there is more yet to be done. People who display negative emotion are often labelled as difficult yet if you move past the emotional reaction and interpret the reasons behind the reaction, you can resolve the problems.

## Handle communication failure

Communication is necessary for a team to function properly. Wrong choice of words and tone of voice can send the wrong signal. Learn to communicate clearly by picking the right words in a way that encourages dialogue. Model good communication to your team in order to create a stress-free work environment.

## Understanding group dynamics

Groups can develop cliques in such a way that any addition of a new member results in conflict. To resolve group conflicts, you need to understand each member's role and their perceptions of each other.

## Know your role

Sometimes conflict could be as a result of your own actions. Most people, however, focus on the role of others in the conflict and assume they are innocent. Evaluate your behaviour and see if there is anything that could have resulted in the conflict.

# When two people come to you for help

Sometimes conflict between two people requires a third party to resolve. When people seek your assistance in conflict resolution, you can use the following methods to resolve it.

**Arbitration**- give each party a chance to state their case then determine who is right and who is wrong.

**Mediation**-create an environment where the two parties can communicate and create solutions that meet both needs.

**Negotiation**-give both parties a chance to float possible solutions till they arrive on one that is a compromise.

**Counselling**-listen to the issues at hand with an empathetic ear without offering any solutions.

Mediation.

If you choose mediation, use the following steps to get a solution.

**Plan and set up the meeting**

Determine the parties involved in the conflict, the issues at hand and then invite the parties to a meeting. In addition, ensure the meeting area is comfortable and offers privacy.

**Give the ground rules**

Explain the expectations and ground rules such as common courtesy. Explain your role clearly as a neutral facilitator.

## Share perspectives

Give each party a chance to explain the conflict from their perspective and reframe it to ensure that the facts are clear.

## Create the agenda

Give the parties a chance to create discussion points and keep the discussion focused on the listed topics.

## Negotiate in good faith

Listen to all the ideas that they come up with and explore the impact of each making sure each party understands the impact of their suggested solutions.

## Where necessary meet each party separately

If the parties are too angry to have a productive discussion together, meet them separately and find out what the issues are. In addition, have them commit to dong a few things in the spirit of progress.

## Create agreements

Once you've met each party privately, bring them together and let them share the discoveries made in the private sessions. Narrow down to specific solutions and have them commit to an agreement that clearly states what each will do as well as the timelines for the implementation.

**Follow up**

Monitor progress to ensure that they are on track in implementing the agreement.

## Fighting fair in your relationships

Conflict is inevitable in relationships. It can make or break a relationship, however, depending on how it is handled. Below are tips to fight fair and keep the relationship.

**Accept conflict**

Some people grow up thinking conflict is a negative thing that ought to be avoided. Conflict is normal and healthy. In a relationship, conflict provides an opportunity for growth and intimacy. If you are open to conflict, it allows you to raise the issues at hand and learn the other person's perspective. This in turn deepens your relationship.

**Fight the issue not the other person**

No matter how hurt or angry you feel, remember, your partner or friend simply did something wrong but they aren't evil or malicious. It is easy to attack the other person when hurt and this can cause scars that can't be undone. Always remind yourself why the relationship with the other person matters to you and thus deal with the issue not the person.

## Stick to the issue at hand

Forget about the thing they did ten years ago that hurt you, even if it's the same as what they just did. It's tempting to gather 'dirt' on the other person to prove your point but it only takes the argument off track and you end up not resolving anything.

## Don't hide under certain topics; deal with the issue

You may find yourself fighting over different things and the fights landing on the same issue. Don't be afraid to tackle the actual issue. If you need acknowledgement or reassurance or a simple apology; stop picking a fight over a towel on the floor. Let your partner know exactly what you need. It may require you to get vulnerable but the results will be an improved relationship.

## Don't downplay the issue

When your partner raises an issue, validate or acknowledge it even if it appears petty to you. Ignoring an issue won't make it go away, it will only magnify it.

## Don't build walls or chase

Silent treatment kills relationships. You can take a break to cool down and think through the issue but withdrawing and hiding behind a wall will only damage the relationship. Attacking serves the same purpose; it destroys the relationship. Find a way to express your feelings without attacking.

**Don't expect your partner to read your mind**

The other person cannot read your mind. It is up to you to explain what the issue is. Ironically most people expect their partners to know what the issue is and when the partner is clueless, they feel neglected and get angry. On the other hand, avoid reading your partner's mind. It's controlling and results in a shutdown of communication.

**Understand the reason behind the anger**

Anger does not exist alone; it's as a result of other underlying emotions. If you can find the real emotion behind your anger, you'll be better placed to respond to the real issue. The same applies to your partner, pay attention when your partner is angry; it will help you pick up clues on what's really going on.

**Pay attention**

Failing to give the other person attention during conflict is simply rude. What is likely to happen when your partner discovers your lack of attention is that the conflict will become about the way you don't care and the issue will be abandoned.

**Don't shout**

When one person starts shouting, the argument can quickly escalate into a shouting match. Nobody gets heard and the issue remains unresolved yet the wounds of hurt only get deeper. If the argument degenerates into yelling, one person needs to be the bigger person and calm down or take a break till everyone calms down.

### Don't label

Labelling your partner by using terms such as 'you never' or 'you always' is counterproductive. It makes them defensive and your issue gets lost.

### Seek more information

Instead of listening while formulating your response, seek more information. When you ask for details, it shows that you are open to resolving the issue.

### Realize that the other person is human

Acknowledging that the other person is not perfect will make it easier to resolve the conflict. This is because being imperfect gives room for mistakes.

### Don't be passive-aggressive

Pretending to be soft while being sarcastic or being brutally honest to the extent of hurting the other person only makes things worse.

### Apologize

If you are on the wrong just apologize.

### Learn to compromise

There is a saying that 'you can either be right or be in a relationship.' You can't be right all the time and keep the relationship alive. You need to find common ground where everybody wins.

**Resolve the issue**

Don't leave issues hanging; press on till you find closure.

# Teaching children conflict resolution

The earlier your children learn how to resolve conflict, the easier their relationships will be. When teaching, timing is of paramount importance. Children generally don't respond well when they are hungry, tired or in a hurry. Start with something that lightens their mood such as a game. In addition, choose a place that is private and comfortable for them. Furthermore, choose a time when you are in your best mood. Handling kids requires a lot of patience which you will not possess if you are irritable or tired.

# Teaching styles

The style you choose should be based on your child's age and personality.

**Modelling**

Modelling is a powerful method. Children model their parents' behaviour more than they obey. To teach your child anger management, you need to learn to control anger so that they can model that.

**Direct teaching**

Most parents choose direct teaching as it's the easiest route. All you need to do is give instructions on what you expect your child to do. While this style carries the danger of your child blocking you to avoid lecturing, it does work for some children. It is structured and specific which makes it easy for kids to relate certain situations with the parent's expectations. Be careful with the timing and mood and keep the instructions short and specific as children have a short concentration span.

## Making good behaviour stick

Once you've taught your child the right method to resolve conflict, you'll want the skills to stick. Here's how you can help your child retain the good behaviour while letting bad behaviour go.

**Positive reinforcement**

Children thrive when their parents are happy. Opportunities for positive reinforcement will arise in the course of the day's activities, take advantage and let your child know when you notice good behaviour. In addition, you could introduce rewards as a form of reinforcement. You can involve your child in choosing the appropriate reward for good behaviour. For most children, the following things will work as reinforcement:

Giving them the privilege to choose what to do with their time

Playing with them as they enjoy your company

Paying attention to what they are doing as it makes them feel cared for.

Recognizing when they shine and succeed.

**Withholding attention**

Sometimes punishment is needed to reinforce good behaviour. Children crave emotional attention and a good relationship with their parents. Sometimes, withdrawing the attention is enough punishment to set them on the right path. If you plan to use attention withdrawal as punishment, be sure to offer loads of attention when they do the right thing. If you don't give your child enough attention, they may resort to negative behaviour to get you to notice them so balance is key.

**Point system**

This is a system where parents award points to children for meeting their daily goals. The goals can be two to four but not more to avoid an overload. At the end of the day, the parents and children go over the daily goals and award each child points based on their performance. The children can also earn additional points depending on how they handle feedback. At the end of the week, rewards are given based on the accumulated points. This system teaches children that every action no matter how small counts and it contributes to a bigger picture.

## When to get help

While conflict is normal, sometimes it goes too far and law enforcement officers need to get involved.

It is important to recognize signs of abuse so that you can get help. They include:

**Verbal abuse and insults-** if the person keeps calling you names threatening and mocking you, constantly, you are in an abusive relationship.

**Manipulation-** if the person is constantly threatening to self-harm report you to the police, or withdraw privileges while lying to the people who matter to you to make you look bad; its abuse.

**Disrespect-** being put down in public, humiliation and taking money without asking is abuse.

**Harassment-**when a person is stalking you, checking up on you and invading your privacy; they are abusing you.

**Threats-** when a person keeps threatening to harm you or destroys your property, they are in actual sense abusing you.

**Physical and sexual violence-**no matter how bad a conflict gets, nobody should shove, punch or push you. Furthermore, no one should touch you in a sexually suggestive manner or talk to you about sex against your will. That amounts to abuse.

When relating with a person who can't control their anger and keeps resorting to crying and begging to get your forgiveness while not making any effort to change, third party intervention is your only hope.

Abuse should be reported to the person who has authority to stop it.

## Why people misuse you

You feel guilty about disputes

Keep in mind, impossible people aren't so impossible when you can prepare for precisely what they're going to state or do next.

Before you deal with somebody, initially be truthful about why you've decided to challenge them about the concern. All too typically, people either avoid the problem or manage it in awkward, insufficient ways. Also, remember that you do not need to deal with everybody as making an issue from everything will just develop unwanted stress.

Many individuals are anxious when it comes to getting into a fight. The best plan is to have that fictional conversation in your head; so you can plan precisely what you want to say and how you'll say it.

When we challenge somebody, we normally have all of it played out in our minds. We go through precisely what each person will mention and respond and how the result will perhaps end up. The guts to challenge is an act of appreciating oneself enough to stand firm on precisely what you prefer and believe without getting caught up in the concern of others' feelings. Consider exactly what specific outcome you'd like to see, such as the person stopping an unfavourable habit, begin more favourable behavioural modifications or make some other adjustment. Keep that goal in mind, when you face the person.

Know exactly what you are going to state ahead of time. Focus on exactly what has taken place resulting in you getting upset and explain your reasoning.

Perhaps there is something for you to find. If they react with anger or aggression, be gentle but nevertheless firm in your position. You will definitely feel happy with yourself, if you can be clear and honest, even if the outcome isn't really what you hope it would be.

you may have found yourself having spent hours tossing and turning in bed during the night having dream conversations with people with whom you are upset with. Not only does this practice interrupt your sleep, your mindset and your health, it never ever in fact handles the issue, and is possibly hazardous to your relationships since you're harbouring inner anger.

Many individuals tip-toe around challenging individuals instead of handling the problems head on. Instead of postponing the confrontation with these individuals, face them directly ASAP!

I'm not suggesting that we go around informing everyone exactly what we think of them all the time; neither am I promoting creating negativity in your relationships over little issues. Nevertheless, what I'm saying is that if you truly feel mistreated by somebody else, you are the individual accountable for making them conscious. It assists us all when aspiring to teach each other to be better and we should not shy away from it due to the fact that it is painful or uncomfortable.

Being sincere with yourself

Setting boundaries and correct limitations remains in reality an act of compassion. By defining your requirements and sensations, you offer others clear and helpful details about how you work and exactly what you need. Being assertive reduces perplexing obscurity.

Figure out precisely what you want deep down. Be particular about what you wish to obtain from a particular discussion or meeting. A vital part of assertiveness is taking inventory of your very own requirements and desires. When you are assertive, you are direct and sincere with individuals. You speak instead of waiting for people to read your mind about what you want. If something is bothering you, you speak out; if you prefer or require something, you ask.

## You are a people pleaser

They're piece of cakes and perennial People Pleasers of society. Good Guys have a difficult time stating no to demands even unreasonable ones. When they want or require something, they hesitate to ask for it because they don't want to hassle others.

Passivity. Trademarks of a passive social strategy consist of waiting for someone else to speak up for them, or hoping that somebody will in some way sense their requirements or experiences. To put it simply, they anticipate individuals to be mind readers!

Being assertive is an essential sort of self-expression.

If you can you scrape underneath the surface area, you will frequently find a defenceless, nervous, and resentful core. Nice Guys are often full of tension and stress and anxiety given that their self-respect relies on the approval of others and getting everyone to like them. They waste a great deal of time attempting to find ways to say no to individuals but typically still end up saying yes.

Another error that people make, especially those who are passive, is believing that they do not have a lot of options when it comes to the way they act. It can be really challenging to simply inform somebody what you desire. You don't need to beat around the bush or anticipate people to read your mind about exactly what you want. It is important to realize that sometimes you are going to upset people. It's a part of being human

## Learning to be assertive

Keep in mind that in some cases it is needed to state what is on your mind as it is more damaging if you keep it within. And, if you are seeking to change something, it's practically a requirement as the majority of things do not move unless they are obliged to.

Assertiveness likewise needs an understanding that while you can make a demand or state an opinion, others are well within their right to say no or disagree. You ought not to get upset when that happens. You remain in control and work to come to some sort of compromise.

Don't hesitate to be more forceful when the circumstance requires it.

Another error that individuals make, especially those who are passive, is believing that they do not have many choices when it comes to how they ought to act. This is absolutely inaccurate. You are a human who has a right to your own body or mind, and you can act in any manner you want within reason.

Assertiveness provides you a voice without compromising yourself or your relationships. Being more assertive first needs you to alter your mind set. You need to eliminate any restricting or incorrect beliefs that are holding you back from being assertive.

Assertive people have the tendency to be the masters of this art. When they feel someone is treating them unfairly, they can let this be known without resorting to aggressiveness. Being too mental in business is continuously a bad thing. You should have the ability to discuss your terms in a way that is concise and clear.

Passive-Aggressive. This behaviour is, where you state one thing and imply another, or you mask your anger and hostility in sarcasm or other hidden communications, in the hopes your concealed attacks will change others. It seldom works and only alienates people from you.

When you feel that you "cannot control the method you act," other people will gladly manage you. Individuals who are aggressive are regularly well-known for having bad moods. It takes little to make them blow up, and if they even believe you are disrespecting them, they will certainly let you know it, typically in an aggressive method.

When you are assertive, you are, by meaning, not "upsetting". Even when you are completely assertive, not in the least offensive, some sensitive individuals are in some cases offended anyway.

## Guidelines for being Assertive

Decide where your limitations lie

We can cut people some slack in life, but please choose just how much you want to take. Know that forgiveness can make the situation even worse if you do not proactively face the issue.

Speak from a position of intelligence and neutrality.

Be confident nevertheless not excessively so. Certainly you wish to be favourable in whatever way when you're being assertive, nevertheless don't attempt so hard to expose your high level of self-esteem that you turn others off and come off as ill-mannered and snobbish.

Remember your objective. Don't take things too personally. Sometimes it can be hard to be assertive since you are frightened that you are going to distress the other person and they might end up not liking you. If you are a people pleaser, this will be particularly frightening for you.

## How to let a difficult person know that their behaviour is wrong if they don't believe it

It is easy to tell someone that they hurt you when what they did is universally accepted as a wrong. But what if they don't think they did something wrong? How then do you convince them that they are wrong?

**Be authentic**

Be truthful. People will not buy what you are saying if it's laced with half-truths. Base your argument on reality and you will get their attention.

**Collect evidence**

When dealing with a person who doesn't hold the same opinion as you, you will need to do your homework. People hold on to beliefs due to the existence of evidence to support them. Prepare by gathering strong evidence to support your opinion for the other person to believe you.

**Use facts to back up your argument**

Difficult people respond better to statistics and numbers as well as findings from respected researchers than repetitions and arguments based on feelings.

**Use social proof**

Use examples of other people who bear the same beliefs as you to show the person that their beliefs are odd. Using social proof works because when in doubt, most people tend to go with the majority.

**Keep repeating the argument**

Repeat the argument over and over again at different strategic times. If you can get others especially people the person respects to do the same, you'll be at a better position to change the person's mind. Try using people that the person respects to propel your argument.

## Get your team to follow your lead

If you don't make a direct demand, then they cannot directly say "no" to you and they also do not get the chance to say "yes". This means that your communication has failed!

If you are trying to get other individuals to do things for you, or to do things you desire for them to do, and you are aiming to fool them to have them do i "out of their own accord", then - sorry to break it to you - there is a probability that you are going to get caught in your efforts at trickery. The truth of the matter is that a few of your requests, indirect as they are, will be annoying. Sometimes, individuals are prepared to trouble themselves to please your request, at other times they will not.

Know your preferred outcome. If you are not actually sure of your personal goals plainly, it will definitely be harder to obtain exactly what you want from the scenario. Believe for a while about what you hope will take place. You'll be more clear-headed during the circumstance, if you do a little mental preparation.

Have clear limitations in mind. In a circumstance where you are being asked to do something with which you aren't a comfy with, understand what it costs, what you are going to do and exactly what would be going too far.

Rehearse what you are going to do. If you practice saying exactly what you prefer to say ahead of time, you'll have the ability to remain cool throughout the discussion.

Plan to be uncomplicated. It can be truly challenging to simply notify someone what you prefer, specifically if being good to individuals is amongst your more powerful qualities. For some, it appears ill-mannered to state exactly what you think, however in reality it isn't actually disrespectful at all. Avoiding will make you seem passive, weak and spineless.

Attempt to expose yourself clearly nevertheless calmly so that people understand precisely where you stand. Bear in mind that the important thing is to make your viewpoint understood, and back up it.

After mentioning exactly what you desire, the difficult part might be holding your ground if the other person disagrees. Continue the discussion in the same calm, gathered tone, however do not pull back.

Avoid letting your emotions reach a boiling point. Keep a calm demeanour. Respect begets Respect. When you are talking with others, treat them with the very same regard that you would want to be treated with. Imagine that it is your mother or granny that you are aiming to speak with and exercise the same rules.

You'd be surprised at the type of resistance you will encounter when you are assertive! It helps if you can expect when and how individuals will press back during the conversation with you.

 Start small. Much like any brand-new capability, it helps if you begin with something low-stakes then slowly move up.

Typical mistakes many people make that are on the course to being more assertive is to attempt to be assertive all the time. Assertiveness is situational and contextual. You don't always have to defend your rights. Often you simply need to surrender your power and provide what they want. This develops a sense out of availability and dispute.

Stop being a people pleaser. It's impossible to please everyone, all the time, or maybe most of the time, so it's never too late or too early to stop your people-pleasing mindset.

Find ways to Say No- If you do not have the desire to something that others desire you to do, don't hesitate to say no.

Get used to the discomfort of stating exactly what you think and pursuing exactly what you want.

## How to gain respect from difficult people

**Be assertive**

People will not treat you as you deserve but as you demand. If you are accepting door mat treatment, people will walk all over you. Learn to stand up for yourself without necessarily fighting back. This will give you power against difficult people.

**Have accomplishments**

Success will grant you power. Your accomplishments speak for you. Everyone respects the person who can get the job done. Work to get to be the best but don't flaunt your success, allow others to notice it instead. That is real power!

## Be Knowledgeable

There is a saying that 'knowledge is power.' It's true! Possessing knowledge on a particular subject, general intellectual prowess or simply being up to date with what is happening around you gives you power. People generally respect knowledgeable people as they feel inferior to them. Gaining knowledge is not hard but requires some work. You may need to read more or just have a candy dish on your desk. People will repay the generosity with information which could prove useful in the long run.

## Build your network

You don't need to know the senior most person, you only need to know the right one. Treat everyone with decency and fairness and you will earn trust and respect. Genuine relationships will give you legitimate power.

## Take initiative

Taking action will earn you power and influence but only if it's calculated and the right move in the situation. Learn to take in details and don't be afraid to act if you know you are doing the right thing.

## Influence

Communication is central in influencing people. Negotiation and persuasion skills are necessary if you want to win people over. In addition, become a good listener. Listening enables you to know the things that matter to others. With this information, you can persuade them with ease.

The authors, publishers, and distributors of this guide have made every effort to ensure the validity, accuracy, and timely nature of the information presented here However, no guarantee is made, neither direct nor implied, that the information in this guide or the techniques described herein are suitable for or applicable to any given individual person or group of persons, nor that any specific result will be achieved The authors, publishers, and distributors of this guide will be held harmless and without fault in all situations and causes arising from the use of this information by any person, with or without professional medical supervision The information contained in this book is for informational and entertainment purposes only It not intended as a professional advice or a recommendation to act

No part of this book may be reproduced or transmitted in any form whatsoever, electronic, or mechanical, including photocopying, recording, or by any informational storage or retrieval system without express permission from the author

# Other books you might be interested in.

Self Help CBT Cognitive Behavior Therapy Training Course & Toolbox: Cognitive Behavioral Therapy Book for Anger Management, Depression, Social Anxiety, OCD, Sleep Disorders, Addictions, Fears & more

The Art of Erasing Emotions: Techniques to discharge any emotional problems in men, women and children using EFT and Sedona

Aging Strong with Grace

Meditation Power Techniques Course: A beginner's guide to meditation for children, teens and adults

The Ultimate Journal Writing Book for Kids & Adults: learn Ideas, tips, techniques & exercises including journaling's therapeutic powers through daily personal self dialogue, prompts/questions etc...

Personal Life Motivation Skills Manifesto: The best self help book to push the motivational switch on how to self motivate, keep yourself motivated, beat lack of drive or no motivation in men & women

How to Improve Emotional Intelligence: the best coaching, assessment & action book on working & developing high eq emotional intelligence quotient mastery of the full emotional intelligence spectrum

The Ultimate Book for Overcoming Dyslexia - Tools for Kids, Teenagers & Adults: A dyslexia empowerment plan & solutions tool kit for tutors and parents to provide dyslexia help for kids & adults

Made in United States
Orlando, FL
15 December 2021

11781935R00039